Staying Sane

99 Ways To Stop Yourself Going Mad
When You Become A Mother

Staying Sane

99 Ways To Stop Yourself Going Mad
When You Become A Mother

KATHY MILLER
Illustrations by Louise Quirke

PORTICO

First published in Great Britain in 2007 by
Portico Books
10 Southcombe Street
London
W14 0RA

An imprint of Anova Books Company Ltd.

ISBN 9781906032012

10 9 8 7 6 5 4 3 2 1

Printed and bound by MPG Books Ltd, Bodmin, Cornwall.

This book can be ordered direct from the publisher.
Contact the marketing department, but try your local bookshop first.

www.anovabooks.com

About the Author

Kathy Miller came to motherhood late and via a circuitous route. Having spent nearly ten years with the BBC as a copy-writer, publicist and radio researcher, she then joined ITN, where she shared the role of Head of Publicity, spending the rest of her working week as a freelance journalist, writing for many national newspapers. At the age of 38, however, she gave it all up to stay at home with her children.

Kathy was educated at Watford Grammar School for Girls and Durham University. She has worked in France, Germany, Spain and America, but now lives in Hertfordshire with her husband and three gorgeous young daughters – and does her best to stay sane.

Acknowledgements

Writing a book about motherhood has been an absolute pleasure but I could not have done it without the tremendous encouragement I received all along from my agent, Charlotte Vamos of IMP and my publisher, Tom Bromley at Portico – both of whom were such fun to work with.

I am also enormously grateful to Helen Ponting and Malcolm Croft, also at Portico, for their endless patience and good humour and to Louise Quirke for her lovely illustrations.

I am deeply indebted to my parents, Rosamond and Douglas Miller, for sharing so much wisdom on the art of parenting and for being such loving and hard-working grandparents.

My thanks also go to my brothers Tom and Stephen and to Theresa Ross, for all their babysitting.

There are many children, in addition to my own daughters, whose antics provided so much source material for this book. In particular, I would like to mention my god-daughters Helena Britten and Hilary Howson and their sisters, and my nephew James Miller.

There are many mothers – and some fathers – whose conversations, heard, overheard (and possibly misheard) made their way into this book. Many of them are great friends, but they are too numerous to thank individually. Without them, however, this book could never have been written.

Last, but by no means least, I want to thank my husband Chris, for his love and support, and for keeping me sane.

For
Philly, Lucy and Marina

CONTENTS

Introduction

If giving birth felt as if I'd shifted an articulated lorry with a roof-rack and a tow-hook, *actually caring* for a baby (twins in my case) made me feel like a tube of toothpaste that had been run over by the Chelsea tractor belonging to Supermum next door.

It was winter, my daughters had been born six weeks early and were healthy but tiny. Two-hourly feeds meant that I barely left the house for three months and the only local person I knew was our postman, George.

I realised that I might be losing my grip when party workers rang me to enquire about my voting intentions in the forthcoming General Election and I was so grateful for their conversation that in the end, *they* hung up on *me.*

In short, the happiest event of my life was also proving to be the toughest.

Fortunately, the entirely unscientific research that I have carried out since then has convinced me that I was not unique in feeling this way.

In life BC (before childbirth), a woman might succeed in running a department and managing huge sums of money and yet still find time to go to the gym twice a week.

In life AD (after delivery), however, motherhood is more difficult than most of us ever believed possible.

Sleep-deprived and with a baby in tow, merely going to the supermarket feels like a polar expedition and following a recipe as easy as studying for a PhD in applied physics.

Instead of writing proposals and drawing up budgets, you now find yourself wandering aimlessly around the house in your dressing-gown, stopping only to stare hollow-eyed at an empty fridge or watching daytime television, because it's marginally better than staring at an empty fridge. But only just.

And now, precisely when you can barely understand the instructions on a microwave meal, you get presented with parenting books the size of telephone directories – that you will *never* find time to read.

Staying Sane offers an antidote to such manuals. I have tried to fill it with pithy little gems on the ups and downs of motherhood, in order to reassure you that you are not the only one driven to distraction by being cooped up at home.

I have also tried not to lecture you on you how to be the perfect mother. Instead, I hope *Staying Sane* will provide you with at-a-glance nuggets of wisdom and humour to help you get through the darkest days of maternal dementia. I trust it will even help you con your husband into thinking he's getting a decent meal every night.

Please keep this book under your pillow or pop it into your handbag to flick through while you're waiting to see the officious health visitor at the baby clinic. Laugh at the bits you find entertaining, show your other half the tips you think he could use and pour your sanity-saving, pre-dinner tipple over the entries that don't apply.

Author's Note

As you read *Staying Sane*, you will notice that I use the word *husband*.

There are of course many other terms I could have used for the man who was (ir)responsible for your maternal state. (I could for instance have opted for *significant other, partner, boyfriend, father of your child* – the list goes on and on. Personally, I would have preferred the word *lover*, but my *better half* wouldn't let me.)

Please be assured that my use of *husband* is not an indication of prejudice on my part. I just happen to be married to the father of my children and for the sake of *my* sanity, I have kept things simple by using the same noun throughout. If you don't like the word *husband*, I positively encourage you, in the cause of *your* sanity, to put a line through it and substitute whichever word you prefer.

Similarly, because all three of my offspring are female, I have tended to refer to children as *daughters* rather than *sons* and use the pronouns *she* and *her* more frequently than *he* and *his*. Again, just get out your red pen if you are the mother of boys – and be grateful that your husband (or *other half*, *bloke*, etc) will find a son easier to dress than a daughter.

Living With Shell Shock

Should you keep the baby
or send it back?

Staying Sane

1 You bring the baby home, your stitches feel like barbed-wire knickers and you make the heart-breaking discovery that your husband is in love with someone else. He thinks about her all day long, goes all gooey whenever she is mentioned and asks fondly after her on the phone. He even goes to see *her* before *you* every evening.

You have two solutions: (i) you take up martial arts; (ii) you buy a negligée and smother yourself in Chanel Number 5. (Either way, you get to pin your husband to the floor.)

Whatever your preference, insist that your husband speaks to you, and you alone, for five whole minutes when he gets in at the end of each day. Only then can he go to see his darling baby daughter.

Staying Sane

2 An indignant Aunt rings you late at night to tell you that she hasn't heard from you in ages and asks 'Is everything all right?'. In other words, you haven't written to thank her for her baby present. You feel like hitting her …

Instead, keep a stock of small thank-you cards so that *your husband* can acknowledge gifts promptly and succinctly (and thus ensure that your second baby gets presents too).

Make it easy for him by keeping a list of which gift was sent by whom. You don't want him to thank your most stylish friend for a miniature china teddy when she actually sent your baby an exquisitely tasteful garment from Paris. Neither do you want to find that he has written to donor of said teddy, thanking her for a beautiful dress and regaling her with a tale of how a hideous china teddy went straight to the charity shop.

3 A rich relative comes up with a huge cheque to celebrate your new arrival. Put it towards a dishwasher and a tumble-drier. You will soon find yourself using both so often that you feel you should give them a cap and pinny and a draughty bedroom in the attic. We rely on ours so heavily that we call them Mary and Elizabeth. (As in: '*What a delicious meal that was. Now ring the bell and call for Mary.*' Or, as my husband might say: '*Why hasn't Elizabeth ironed my shirt?*')

Staying Sane

4

Feeling sluggish and drowsy? Really? Come on, keep those energy levels high by running up and down stairs at each nappy change! Tone your biceps by carrying the baby dumb-bell style, as you sprint up and down! Hey, get real and be kind to yourself. Keep a supply of nappies and wet wipes upstairs *and* down and resign yourself to being chubby for a while longer.

But just because you're flabby on the outside doesn't mean you shouldn't be taut and toned on the inside. Force yourself to do pelvic floor exercises each time you change a nappy. Make a reminder for yourself and pin it above your baby's changing-mat.

(Alternatively, you could join a gym with a crèche, or even employ a personal trainer, preferably a tall, T-shaped one named Sven or Pierre.)

5 Looking distinctly undesirable in your husband's baggy sweater? Give yourself an air of glamorous mystery by wrapping your head in a pashmina. That way you need never have a bad-hair day and you can drape the shawl nonchalantly over yourself and the baby when you are breast-feeding in public.

6 Murphy's Law for Mums says that when you fancy a stroll with the pram, you struggle to get tiny hands and feet into a pastel-coloured space suit and hey presto, you smell a poo (two poos if you have twins) and you have to start all over again, only by now, the sky looks ominously grey. Save time by swaddling the baby in a warm blanket.

7

Ever wondered what it felt like to own a Rolls Royce? Want to get chatting to strange men? Buy an old-fashioned second-hand pram and go for a walk whenever it's fine. The baby will appreciate the fresh air and unfamiliar sights and because she is facing you, she will smile and gurgle so delightfully that you forgive her everything. (There is even some research to suggest that you could be laying the foundations for an exceptionally articulate adult in her later years.)

As for you though, it will feel as if you're driving a top-of-the-range car and like a dog, a real pram is a great talking point.

8 Of course, you could actually get a dog.
A Rottweiler to be specific. Appoint a
human guard-dog to frighten away any
unwanted guests when you first come
home with the baby. Your own mother
is probably best, but if you
get on with your mother-
in-law, this can work
well too. Just make
sure that whoever
you choose knows
that while she is in
your house, *she* is cooking/shopping/cleaning for
you, not the other way round.

Staying Sane

9 If you can't abide dogs (or your mother-in-law), keep a dressing-gown by the front door to don quickly in order to discourage unwanted callers. (Just remember that jeans poking out underneath are a bit of a giveaway.) And when you do invite people round to admire the new addition to the family, insist that they arrive at a time that suits you – not so that you can plump up the cushions or bake shortbread – but so that whatever rest you are managing to get, is not interrupted.

10 Vomit, sick, puke, chunder … it finds its way into the most unlikely places. Just ask anyone who valets cars for a living. (Under the seats, into the inside door pockets, down the little recesses where the seat belts are secured, in case you were wondering.) For children over the age of two, there are several travel sickness syrups available. Until then you must prepare yourself for the worst your baby can throw up at you. Get yourself a ruck-sack and fill it with everything you need to change a vomit-covered infant (and feed and entertain her in a 10-mile tail-back on the M25). Keep this 'Magic Bag' ready-packed behind your front door so that you can grab it at a moment's notice.

11 Some mothers (and I suspect, most fathers) are happy to feed their baby *Ifit* every day. (Author's translation of *Ifit*: *If it's in the fridge, she's having it…*) If you are not one of these parents, you need a reputable infant cookery book. You know, one of those brightly illustrated tomes on weaning for gourmet babies, the one that every mother has, but rarely uses? *Come on*, you must have it somewhere, the one with an immaculately coiffeured blonde Mummy on the front cover? Simply identify the five simplest recipes for your baby's solids and stick to them, Monday to Friday. You can give yourself a break at the weekend by using food from jars or packets. (Assuage any guilt by buying the organic stuff.)

Staying Sane

12 If you are saintly enough to make your own baby food for the freezer, buy those rubber ice-cube trays that pop the contents out without breaking your finger nails. Be sure to catch the flying cubes in a bowl or cup, otherwise you could find your lovingly prepared frozen organic parsnip purée skidding across the kitchen floor.

13

The French do everything so much better, don't you agree? Food, wine, *couture*, lurve ... well, when it comes to helping your baby sleep, the French win first prize *encore*. If you haven't yet discovered the dinky little-sleeping bags that the French use for their infants, buy one now. These wonderful straitjackets are *absolument magnifiques* (and available from most UK department stores). Not only do they keep even the most mobile of babies contained in the cot, they keep the baby warm, and thus quiet, all night long, because she can't kick the *turbulette* off. *C'est formidable, n'est-ce pas?*

(Author's advice: when trying to remember the French term *turbulette*, think *turbulent baby* and you won't go far wrong.)

Staying Sane

14 If you thrived on pressure in your career, chances are you will find motherhood, with its seemingly endless days when nothing actually gets done, but you have no time to do it in, *pretty mundane*. Give yourself a sense of achievement by making a list of 'Things To Do', what you might call a domestic in-tray. For example:

Change 6 nappies
Make 2 ice-cube trays of vegetable purée
Pay credit card bill over phone
Walk round block with pram

Cross each one off as you get there and award yourself stars if you over-achieve.

Changed 8 nappies. Two gold stars!

You could even remind yourself of the joys of office life by setting yourself deadlines, thus:

Before lunch: Apply lipstick (and mascara if time)
Sometime this afternoon: Watch 30 minutes of daytime telly
5-ish: Phone husband to ask if he wants spaghetti hoops or cheese on toast for supper.

15

It is OK not to like other women, honestly. Just because you have a child, doesn't mean that you have to make instant friends with everyone at your nearest Mums and Babies group. If you don't hit it off with the group, ask around about others (your health visitor or doctor will have a list). If you are a member of a minority (you have twins, say, or are American), you will almost certainly find a group that actually specialises in odd-balls like you. It will help you to feel normal again if you can meet other mothers with whom you have more in common than just a baby.

16 If you have a garden, hang your washing on the line in good weather. Even a short blast of air or sunshine will lift your spirits. Let your baby watch you from his pram or buggy. If he gets bored, improvise a dance routine involving a bra and a tea towel.

17 Gardens also come in handy when you have reached the end of your tether. Treat yourself to a few moments' peace by taking the pram to the bottom of the garden where you can't hear the baby crying and, having made sure that he is securely fastened, leave him there for 10 minutes. Your mother will only now admit she did the same with you, rain or shine 'brushed the snow off the pram...'

18 Don't ever be tempted to drink too much alcohol, especially if you are breast-feeding. Babies are born with a ferociously Puritanical streak and are notoriously unforgiving of their mother's hangovers.

19 So what if your house is a tip and you have vomit on your shoulder? You've just produced a baby for goodness sake, not a self-improvement guide. Learn to see baby sick as a badge of honour! Even so, insist that visitors wash their hands before touching the baby. (They will almost certainly want to wash their hands *afterwards*.) The only time a baby of mine was horribly sick *all night,* was following a cuddle from a friend who had been outside all day, breezed in and stuck her fingers in the baby's mouth – but didn't bother to wash her hands first.

Staying Sane

20 Don't waste your maternity pay on baby paraphernalia unless at least one friend has told you that she found it absolutely indispensable. The best recommendations I received were for a baby gym and a travel cot. The former, because it kept my twins quiet for long enough to allow me to make the odd phone call and the latter because, when downstairs, it made an ideal holding-pen whenever I needed to mop up a sticky, toxic or malodorous substance from the kitchen floor.

And my worst buy? Well, since you asked, it was a (fake) silver box for baby's first tooth or lock of hair. I don't need to explain why this was a complete waste of space and money.

21 Never refuse offers of help. If a friend or neighbour kindly proposes to do something for you, flatter them by accepting graciously. They won't offer again if they are turned down. If a good cook suggests something for your freezer, bite her hand off for it. However, if a lousy cook offers her services, ask her to shop for you instead.

22

You will be horrified by how much confidence you lose within the first few weeks of motherhood. You may suffer from PDSD (post-delivery stress disorder), when even making a short car journey with your baby terrifies you. If you are going somewhere for the first time, try to familiarise yourself with the route and local parking restrictions *before* you take the baby.

Always have with you your 'Magic Bag' (see Tip Number 10), enough small change for the parking meter while you're there, and, if possible, an adult companion to help steady your nerves. (A hip flask of brandy may sound more compelling, but your local bobby might not agree.)

23

When your hands are full of baby and it's raining, you don't want to be rummaging in the bottom of your bag for your keys. Wear your car/house keys around your neck or waist until your baby can walk. Call it your *accessoire à clé*. You never know, it might catch on.

Descent Into Paranoia

Are toddlers human?
Your questions (un)answered

24

Don't get mad, get even! Rehearse the art of embarrassing your toddler, so that you have perfected it by the time he reaches adolescence. Keep a stock of your favourite CDs in your kitchen to gyrate to while waving your oven-gloves in the air. Much loved female anthems in my part of the world are 'I Will Survive' (Gloria Gaynor), 'I Am A Woman In Love' (Barbara Streisand) and 'Dancing Queen' (Abba).

Staying Sane

25 When your toddler 'planks' uncompromisingly on the supermarket floor and you weigh up the attraction of leaving the shop immediately, against the pressing need for a well stocked fridge, think instead of your frustrations with the office photo-copier, the severity of whose mechanical failures was in direct proportion to the urgency of the task required of it. And be jolly grateful that it's only your maternal pride and not a lucrative contract that is at stake.

(Author's translation: *To plank* is to lie rigidly on the floor, usually in a public place and when time is at a premium. In older toddlers, it is often accompanied by violent kicking, demands for sweeties and loud shrieks of '*I hate you Mummy!*')

26

Establish family 'rituals' early on in your child's life. You could encourage her to listen to tapes chosen for specific car journeys e.g. *Just William* pranks for a visit to your maiden Aunt or *Winnie the Pooh* and his overindulgence with *hunny* for the supermarket trip; you might set aside Friday afternoons for any chore which your child can be persuaded is actually a treat, such as cleaning out the hamster's cage. Book Daddy in for bedtime reading at weekends, especially for any story that includes a mention of botty burps and the like … In the short-term, these activities give endless hours of pleasure to small children and can be used as a 'carrot' whenever your relationship with your toddler reaches melt-down. Looking ahead, such family traditions might also provide a huge source of humiliation when trotted out in front of a teenage son's new girlfriend or at his 18th birthday party.

27

Remember when you were child-free and would munch on a piece of toast as you rushed to press a skirt for the office, only to spend all day fretting about having left the iron on by mistake? Well, yippee!

Having a toddler means that now there are two other domestic hazards to drive you mad: (i) hot bath water and (ii) boiling saucepans.

(i) If you don't want a screaming toddler who looks like a fried prawn, put cold water in the bath first and *then* add the hot. It sounds basic, but you will understand by now why the tea-time-bath-time routine is known as 'The Witching-Hour'. It is the most trying part of the day and the only way to get through it is on automatic-pilot, which is *precisely* when you could scald your child by absent-mindedly dipping him into a bath that is positively steaming.

(ii) Similarly, get into the habit of placing saucepans at the back of the stove, with the handles pointing away from you. It's an awful truism, but you don't want to walk into the kitchen to find your toddler lying unconscious under the pan of boiling gravy that he has knocked over.

28

For once, your Mother was right. If car seats had existed in her day, she would have stopped at one child. A car seat becomes a positive assault on your sanity as soon as your child starts to arch his back in protest whenever you try to put him into one. Of course seats save lives, but even so, you will want to strap your toddler into his car seat as infrequently as possible. Do what your Mother would have done and reduce the number of car journeys you make by planning just one type of shop for each day e.g. Monday for the supermarket, Tuesday for baby clothes, Wednesday the butcher, Thursday the baker, Friday the candlestick maker etc. If you want to remind yourself of your working days, you could buy an office-type timetable and schedule your shopping-trips.

29 Even better, walk! Shed that post-pregnancy blubber and embrace the need for daily shopping! Engage with your surroundings! Your daily stroll will become something you look forward to, your toddler will get a change of scene and because you buy only what you can carry or push in the back of the buggy, you will even save money.

30

Best of all, save your legs by getting the milkman to deliver the milk and arrange for a box of organic fruit and veg to arrive on your doorstep each week. Believe it or not, you can still order these over the phone. You could do it electronically of course, but be warned, if you were a Technobimbo BC, your addled toddler-crazed brain AD will be defeated by the intricacies of Internet shopping.

One mother I know went online to order a handbag from a designer calling herself Madame Fifi, only to find herself offered all sorts of 'adult' products. When her husband was surfing the Internet later, he wondered what on earth his wife had been up to. Mind you, he emerged from his stint at the computer with a definite spring in his step!

31 You could allow yourself to feel really virtuous about saving the rain forests by using terry nappies. However, if, like most worn-out mothers, you buy the disposable ones, find the brand that has the same picture on every nappy. A fashion-conscious two-year-old will waste valuable time when you're in a hurry trying to decide between elephants and teddy bears.

And I must advise you that with older siblings, knix with pix (that's *knickers with pictures* if your child has given you a bad night) provoke all kinds of arguments. Just tell your children that when it comes to underwear, they can have any colour they like, as long as it's white.

32

Expect to hate every family holiday you take and you'll be pleasantly surprised. Golden rules for staying sane on holiday are:

(i) Make packing easier by keeping an open suitcase on the spare bed for a week before you go. As each child's garment is washed and dried, put it straight into the case.

(ii) Choose a destination that is under three hours' drive away. If this is impossible, you could opt to drive at night time and pray that the children stay asleep. Or be really intrepid and turn a long journey into an excursion in itself by making a lunchtime detour to a National Trust property en route. (See Tip Number 78 for what membership of this honourable institution can bring you.)

(iii) Find an establishment whose swirly carpet and floral wallpaper can only be improved by projectile vomit and the injudicious use of felt-tip pens.

(iv) If you find the cuisine in the above mentioned hotel inedible, the likelihood is that your kids will love it.

(v) Buy those swimsuits that resemble Edwardian bathing-costumes, in ludicrously bright colours, with in-built buoyancy aids. They protect your children from the sun, help keep them afloat and can be spotted a mile off on a crowded beach.

33

Aim for the impossible: try for 10 minutes 'Special Time' with your child every day. Such time is harder to find than you could ever have imagined, but all you need to do is read to your child. She will love you for it and it will benefit her enormously if she is a slow reader.

34

When you've achieved the impossible (see Tip Number 33), aim for something so easy it's what your former colleagues would have called 'a no-brainer': allow yourself an heretical half an hour in front of the telly each afternoon with your children. You get the most wonderful cuddles, it helps relax all of you and your kids will enjoy asking and answering questions about the programmes.

35 Live dangerously: go to the supermarket *alone* occasionally. Arrange to leave your child with another mother. You will be surprised how liberating this feels and even more surprised to learn how well behaved your child is capable of being without you.

36 Get rid of your husband and your toddler. Pack them off for a couple of hours at the weekend to a local farm, model village, activity centre, zoo etc. Spending money up-front on an annual family pass will encourage you (and them) to use it more often.

Staying Sane

37 Never tell small children where you plan to take them tomorrow, or who they are going to see. They will only be disappointed if it is called off. Tell them instead that they are 'going on an adventure.' Then it won't matter if it's only a trip to Sainsbury's.

38 Do something that you enjoy so much, you almost feel ashamed. My guilty secret came in the shape of pottery and German classes, both of which I started when my youngest daughter attended pre-school. Wednesdays and Fridays became the highlights of my week. As we pummelled and kneaded and bashed our clay, our chats were so *therapeutic*. And as a fellow potter's husband assured me, 'We men may not like what our wives talk about when we're not around, but I'm sure we benefit from the *outworkings* of your discussions.' *Mein Gott*, as the Germans say, how very understanding of him.

39 If you want to make a lifelong friend, compliment another woman on her child's manners, willingness to share or take turns, cleanliness, sense of fair play, taste in Mickey Mouse trainers etc. No matter how intelligent and well-educated the woman, she will believe you and admire you for evermore.

40 If, on the other hand, you want to get rid of a hanger-on, have the audacity to raise your eyebrows when a toddler bashes your little angel over the head with a near life-size model fire engine. You will be struck off his mother's Christmas card list immediately.

(The moral of Tips 39 and 40 is that all mothers are fiercely loyal to their children, however misguided that loyalty sometimes appears to others. The most insincere compliment will be treasured forever, while even the gentlest criticism will be held against you for eternity.)

41

You adore your kids to bits, but you won't always like them. That is OK. Don't beat yourself up about it. Think instead of the ancient Spanish proverb about loving your children so much when they are little that you feel you could eat them – and when they are teenagers you will wish you had.

If you don't want to wait for your child to reach adolescence before using this handy proverb, book a last-minute package holiday to Spain (anywhere in Spain will do) and grab a passing waiter. Point to your planking toddler (see Tip Number 25 for the definition of *planking*) and say: '*Ojalá me lo hubiera comido cuando era bebé*'. (I wish I'd gobbled him up when he was a baby.) The waiter will be so thrilled by this uncharacteristically British attempt to speak his lingo that your child's next ice-cream (and hopefully your next Cuba Libre) will almost certainly be on him.

42 Avoid complete paranoia by resolving to consult a medical dictionary *as rarely as possible* to check up on childhood ailments. Your toddler may only have a runny nose, but peep at the dictionary and you will find that before the day is out, she has developed every symptom of every life-threatening disease you have ever heard of (and plenty you haven't).

Keep a thermometer and all infant medicines in one place (I have found an old ice-cream tub to be best). That way, you know that when you kick your husband out of bed to settle a febrile teething baby, he knows where to find the Calpol.

Total Maternal Dementia

Kidding yourself that
you are OK, really

43

When motherhood seems intolerable, re-read *Bridget Jones's Diary* or *Men Are From Mars, Women Are From Venus*, in order to remind yourself quite how much you disliked being a childless singleton.

44 Whatever your weakness (double whisky, Bacardi Breezer, cooking sherry) keep a stock of the stuff right where you can lay your hands on it – ready mixed in cans in the fridge if necessary. It will restore your sanity and save your time. (But don't get carried away and find that you forget Tip Number 18.)

45 Do you know any real clever clogs who always leave you at a loss for words? Have you ever walked away from a particularly bruising encounter and wished you'd had a ready retort? (Join the club.) Next time a working mother says patronisingly *'How do you stand it? I'd go mad if I stayed at home. At least by working I'm using my brain'*, you now have the perfect put-down:

'Oh, I don't have a brain. . . But that's OK 'cos none of the doctors or lawyers I meet at coffee mornings have brains either.'

If the woman in question has really got up your nose, you could even add: *'Still, I was clever enough to find a man who could keep me.'*

46

Guess what? Women *can* have it all! Motherhood is when you discover the advantages of the Car Office, or as I fondly call mine, the CARO.

All you need to enjoy this inspired invention is a pen that works, a fully charged mobile phone, your diary and address book, a credit card and the back of an old envelope. Oh, and a slumbering infant. If your child has nodded off in the car, try not to wake her. Use the time to sort your life out. A supermarket car park or even a lay-by are the perfect locations from which to organise social events, pay your bills or dash off a best-seller – all from the comfort of your CARO.

Indeed, most of this book got written that way!

47

Discover your inner minx! Make yourself feel racy during the frumpy days of breast-feeding with a naked male fridge magnet! Let off steam by drawing a moustache on a prominently displayed photo of your mother-in-law! Retrieve your mislaid sense of humour by sticking the most fatuous piece of parenting advice you can find on your kitchen notice board. One of my favourites is a gem from Gina Ford, that doyenne of contented babies everywhere, who cautions mothers to avoid talking to, or making eye contact with, their baby at bedtime – which for some reason still makes me laugh even more than my husband's attempts to find matching socks each morning.

48

Arrange to become so demented one weekend that you briefly go AWOL. Nip away for a walk or a coffee. Just go, and don't give your husband much warning. But do leave him a few tips, if only for your children's sake. Left alone one Saturday morning in February while I went to the hairdresser, my dear husband grabbed the first clothes to hand and dressed one baby girl twin in a woolly jumper and tights, (thinking they were leggings), and the other in a cotton sun dress.

49 If Tip Number 48 doesn't work, regain at least some control of the total chaos that is now your life and Get Lost Properly! Push Off Completely! Drive Off In Style! Anywhere. Bundle your daughter into the car (make sure she is clean, dry and fed) and Just Go. While at the wheel you will feel deliciously in charge, (a feeling completely alien to new mothers), your little one will sleep and you will get to lap up adult conversation or soothing music on the car radio.

If you are fortunate enough to live near a common or a park, or close to woods or water, always choose the scenic route for your 'escape.' That way you can remind yourself that it is only because you are a non-working mother that you have the freedom to enjoy such magnificent scenery, miles away from the rush hour traffic.

50

Create a little routine to remind yourself of working life. Make sure it isn't time-consuming or back-breaking and keep it sufficiently simple so that it won't matter if it gets forgotten. Try watering the plants or opening your post at the same time each day. If the routine becomes tiresome, remind yourself that the dazzling career you are missing so badly consisted merely of one routine after another.

51

Get back to your BC figure! It's soooo easy. Just keep a favourite photo of yourself on the fridge or tucked into the bathroom mirror to remind yourself of how damned irresistible you were underneath your post-pregnancy flab. A snap of you looking tanned in a bikini on your honeymoon should do the trick.

52 Too many mothers put on weight by eating up after their children. Save calories by putting a large bowl full of soapy water in the middle of the table and chuck your children's leftovers into it *the moment* they finish their meal. Chewed fish fingers taste even worse when they've been dunked in washing-up liquid. One friend even came up with the slogan: *Never mind the waste, think only of your waist.*

53 Tell all the Mums you know what a dietician friend once told me: eating just one biscuit a day will help them gain half a stone in a year. They will soon stop offering you biccies when you go for coffee.

Get to like rabbit food instead. Keep plenty of carrot and celery sticks in a glass of water on the kitchen sideboard for when you're feeling peckish. If your toddler sees you eating vegetables, she might decide it's cool to do so herself. At least, that's the theory.

Staying Sane

54 Pay a kind teenager or elderly neighbour to come round and entertain your child for a couple of hours one afternoon. Keep out of their way by retiring to bed to listen to a play on Radio 4 or catch up on *Hello!* magazine. If you are self-employed, you may find that your 6-month maternity allowance will cover the cost of an *au pair* for an entire year. My husband could think of countless other ways to spend this little windfall, but as I argued, why shouldn't *my* maternity benefit be put towards *my* maternal benefit?

Staying Sane

55 Get up half an hour early. (That was a joke, by the way.) Some tasks simply cannot be carried out satisfactorily in a kitchen where toddlers are eating Coco Pops and yogurt. If you have a passport application to complete, or if there is an event such as a party or a wedding that you really want to attend, get up early or negotiate half an hour of child-free time with your husband, to type it up, pack your bag etc. You will enjoy the party so much more – and make fewer spelling mistakes – if you do. (On second thoughts, a passport application might require several *days* of child-free time.)

56 Be inventive. Design your own Christmas cards or knit squares for the good ladies of the parish to make into blankets. Perhaps even learn to make jam. (That was another joke, by the way.) Honestly, find an outlet for your creativity. When my twins were tiny, I spent a couple of mornings, with them in the buggy, in a nearby pot-painting studio. The results were dismal, but it cheered me up no end.

57 Keep a journal of your maternal feelings, the highs and lows, peaks and troughs, zeniths and nadirs … Setting aside even a few minutes of diary time each day is a great way to wind down, even if you just write 'bloody awful day, nearly chucked baby out of the window'. Who knows, it might turn into a book on motherhood?

58

Similarly, you could keep a record of your child's development in the rather twee book you will probably have been given for this purpose. The date of your toddler's first tentative steps or words are major milestones at the time, but soon recede into a dim memory unless you write them down. Keep a 'Happy Box' of touching notes you received when you became a Mum, children's drawings, even tapes of baby gurgles – and dip into it when you're feeling stressed. But don't get hung up if your Little Jamie's progress isn't as fast as Little Oliver's next door. *And don't forget that absolutely no one else will be remotely interested in your reminiscences.*

59 If you employ someone to help you with your children, let your husband intervene in any dispute. His approach is bound to be more tactful and therefore more productive, while you might say something you could regret later. However much authority you had in your job, when you're tired or at the mercy of hormones, it is often wiser to let your other half handle delicate negotiations.

Staying Sane

60 Just because you coped with tricky types at work doesn't mean you should do it now. Read the chapter on Mum-upmanship in *Nature's Masterpiece* by Libby Purves, in which she describes several ghastly female stereotypes to watch out for. They are absolutely spot-on. When you're feeling low, Needy Norma, Complacent Carol or Manipulative Maggie (my own bugbears, not Libby's) can drag you down further. Take the rough with the smooth of course, but try to concentrate on women whose company gives you a boost and don't let yourself be undermined by competitive, critical or gossipy women.

61

Be particularly wary of a character I call Saccharine Susie, who will contrive to call into question your ability as a mother by saying horribly spiteful things in the most seemingly innocent way. Such priceless barbs might include:

'How convenient that your children like orange squash. Mine refuse anything containing aspartame.'

Or:

'I know just what you mean about children detesting car seats. We walk everywhere now. It's done wonders for Imogen's road sense.'

(Author's note: Aspartame is an artificial sweetener, something I imagine Saccharine Susie must consume in industrial quantities!)

Staying Sane

62

If you find yourself the victim of Mum-upmanship (see Tip Number 60), get your revenge by making a list called 'All The Things I Hate About Other Mums' and stick it on the fridge whenever you're in need of a laugh. One smug Mary Poppins type once told me, without a hint of irony, that her three-year-old 'just *loves* the pre-Raphaelites'. Underneath this entry on my 'hate' list I wrote, equally seriously 'My toddler simply *adores* lift-the-flap farmyard animal books in primary colours.'

63 Have you ever wondered why men spend so much time in the loo? Take a tip from your husband and seek refuge in the smallest room in the house. Make it as attractive a place as a WC can be; put witty or colourful posters on the walls, a bowl of pot pourri on the window sill, a pile of glossy mages and amusing books (this one, for instance) in a corner, keep a radio in there etc. Lock the door and enjoy a few precious moments to yourself. Your toddler will find you soon enough.

64 As you feel yourself slipping well and truly into insanity, spare a thought for those people who actually do this for a living, rather than people like you for whom full-time motherhood is merely a career break. Think of the nannies, *au pairs* and nursery teachers you know and muse on what twist of fate gave them their vocation and you, yours.

How To Remain Civil To The Man Who Got You Into This Mess

Controlling the homicidal feelings
you are developing towards
your husband

65 When sleep-deprivation has reduced your conversation with your husband to monosyllabic grunts, strap your baby into her car seat and drive, with your other half, to a take-away that is at least a quarter of an hour away. The baby will fall asleep immediately, you will get fifteen minutes of conversation each way and a hot, tasty meal prepared by somebody else. If you give yourselves more time to chat by eating in the car, you may actually like each other by the time you return home.

66 However put-upon you feel, try not to pick a fight with your husband in the evening when you are both shattered. If you really must, do something that bugs him, but which is in itself completely harmless, simply because it makes you feel stronger. For example, my other half hates me drooling over the property ads in *Country Life* because he thinks I will get ideas above my station and start making eyes at the fat rich git down the road. Fortunately for me, my husband daren't complain for fear of looking ridiculous.

Staying Sane

67 Become an exemplary 1950s-style wife and cook your husband something really, really special every evening! May I suggest Monday: lamb chops, Tuesday: frozen fish cakes, Wednesday: gammon steaks with tinned pineapple rings, Thursday: pasta with an exotic sounding sauce (from a jar that you throw away quickly). My, won't he think himself a lucky fella? If you don't advertise the fact that you're working from a rota and you are cunning enough to vary the vegetables, it could be a month before your husband notices that he gets the same thing each week and that you are cooking for your convenience, rather than for his delectation. If he does cotton-on, tell him you're helping him re-live his student days.

68 To hell with the 50's. You're the one who needs a rest. Insist that your husband cooks a meal for you both at least once a week. If he shirks this simple task, eat your own supper early and let him heat up some *Ifit* (see Tip Number 11) for himself. See how long that lasts.

69 When you're texting your husband or leaving a message on his voicemail, don't just give him instructions about picking up a packet of nappies on the way home. Make the messages funny, affectionate, even sexy. Resurrect the nicknames you used when you were courting, tell him you have unearthed the nightie you bought for your honeymoon and will be wearing it tonight (nudge, nudge), or just remind him that you love him. It might feel contrived at first, but it may do wonders for your relationship.

Staying Sane

70

If you've given up a promising career (or just put it on hold), it is easy to think that you have got the raw end of the deal. Maybe you have, but perhaps your husband hates *his* job and would give his right arm to be at home cuddling his baby. It's worth remembering that unlike you, he probably doesn't have a choice in the matter. So be nice to him once in a while.

71

Baby-blues mean that there will inevitably be times when you contemplate the desirability of divorce. The fail-safe solution is to go to a party. *Any party.* Gatecrash one if necessary. It doesn't matter if it's a huge drinks party or an intimate dinner for six, just as long as there is at least one couple whom you haven't met before. Chances are you will have your evening spoiled by a self-important oaf whose prejudices, politics or misogyny ensure that when you snuggle up to your husband in bed that night, you thank your lucky stars that you ended up with *him* (he is the father of your darling baby, after all) and not the other guy. And your husband, who may have got stuck with a neurotic bird-brain all evening, will no doubt feel equally relieved to be married to you.

75

72

Tell your husband that the vacuum cleaner is a power-tool! That dusting is the new sex! Buy disposable dusters and bloke-coloured rubber gloves! However you do it, encourage your husband to do more housework by making it man-friendly. Give him the feeling that he is in control by asking '*Darling, do you want to hang out the baby's clothes or load the dishwasher? Would you prefer to do the ironing or cook supper, my angel?* (You might want to refer back to Tip Number 69 on how to get him in a good mood first.)

73

If your husband is already a domestic god (lucky you) and you are the one who has yet to be house-trained, accept that you will become much worse AD. If this doesn't bother your husband, fine. If it does, try explaining that it is *his* problem, not *yours*. Then agree to compromise by dividing up household duties.

74

On the rare occasions when you manage a 'date' with your husband, steer clear of the dinner *pour deux*. Spending two hours in the exclusive company of a man who has by now become a virtual stranger could degenerate into a long rant about your husband's shortcomings or the injustice of your position, and could even escalate into the sort of row that sends the waiter scurrying for cover. Be realistic; your first meals out together will be something of an anti-climax (rather like a Valentine's Day dinner once you're married). Your time together will be punctuated by long silences and your conversation limited to your baby's bowel movements. Instead, organise a foursome, with people you know well, who are entertaining and easy-going. There will be plenty of time for romantic dinners when you are not so tired.

Staying Sane

75 'Tis The Law Of Sod that the phone will always ring when you're trying to calm the baby, when you're sitting down to supper and the minute you drop off to sleep. It's a lifeline when you're feeling lonely, but when your husband is feeling left-out and desperate for your attention, or when you want a quiet moment with your little one, take the phone off the hook and let the answering-machine deal with your calls.

Discovering That There Is Life AD (After Delivery)

Resuming contact with the outside world and having fun again

76

Indulge your fantasy of a weekend in Paris with a man you lust after (preferably your husband). Start leafing through brochures, brush up your schoolgirl French, practise looking sulkily sexy, buy a beret to wear at a jaunty angle … More prosaically, calculate how much you spend each month on disposable nappies, wet wipes and nappy sacks. Once your children no longer have use for them, put the money into a savings account where you can't get at it. At the end of the year, you will probably have accrued enough cash to take your husband across the Channel for a couple of nights. Just make sure you don't fire out another baby nine months later.

77

While the thought of a weekend in Paris is still a twinkle in your eye, you can always abandon your kids to the care of a friend and discover the joys of 'Daytime Romance'. Get your husband to take the day off, (hands up all those who thought I meant the milkman – shame on you), dress up as if you were on a first date and spend the day together, doing something you really enjoy and couldn't do with children, such as going to an art museum or to see a play.

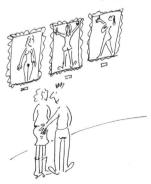

Staying Sane

78 Don't wait until you retire to join the National Trust – Do It Now! You will appreciate the tea room, the shop and the clean loos, while your children will love the gardens and the adventure playground. Always make sure you do something fun as a family on a Bank Holiday. Don't mow the lawn or paint the gutter. Get Out There! In the summer, make twice the amount of whatever you eat the evening before and take it as your picnic for the day out.

79

Revert to being a teenager and work on the assumption that your parents are stupid. (Just don't go the whole hog and start slamming doors and getting spots.) If your mother or mother-in-law offers to have your child for a weekend, don't blow it by presuming too much of her. Ensure that your parents offer to look after your offspring for a *second* time by making it as easy as possible the *first* time. Pack a bag with all the clothes, toys, reading material etc required by your child for the whole period you are away. Leave copious notes on how to work the VCR/DVD, put pre-prepared meals in the freezer, make sure there are enough nappies etc. Do just as you please during your weekend – and then behave like a grown-up and buy Granny some chocolates or flowers afterwards.

Staying Sane

80 As you start to get more time to yourself, so will other Mums. Beware the acquaintance who rings up out of the blue … and gushes about what a long time it's been … and how you must get your kids together … and are you free on Tuesday? You rush to say yes, only to find yourself lumbered with her child for the day while she does lunch, tea and probably dinner with somebody she finds much more interesting than you. Unless you know her well, you will be reticent about asking her to return the favour.

81

Adopt an alias. Pretend you're someone else. Keep an account in your maiden name and while you're not working, arrange for a set sum from your husband's salary to be paid into it by monthly standing order. If you enjoyed financial independence before you had children and find it humiliating to have to ask your husband for extra cash, you will now have a ready supply *that he can't touch*. Obviate any arguments by agreeing beforehand what this money will be used for (preferably on clothes for you, beauty treatments, shoes, handbags etc).

If you can manage it, try putting your child benefit into a tax-free young saver's account. It's a great way to save for your child's future and you will be able to raid it periodically to pay for swimming lessons, school trips, football coaching, ballet classes etc.

82

On the rare occasions you get a chance to read, choose a book that is light, funny and easy to get back into if your child buries it under the sofa for two days. Now is not the time to read *War and Peace*.

83

By the time your children start school, you may be ready to join or form a book club. Make it as intellectual or as raucous as you like. Alternate between the latest blockbuster and the classic you have always promised yourself you would read. You may get to read *War and Peace* after all!

If, like me, you find the idea of an all-female book club too similar to the coffee mornings you have endured almost daily for five years, rope your husband in and get together with a few like-minded couples for a book discussion over dinner one Saturday evening a month. Of course, the men may baulk at the idea of reading Joanna Trollope, but then you may not be wildly enthusiastic about reviewing anything by Dennis Wheatley either.

Staying Sane

84 When you've tried Tip Number 74 and you feel confident that you and your husband are once again on speaking terms, make the most of it. In fact, you can eat out for nothing! Get your babysitting done for free! Once a month, 'dine out' at the home of friends, while they come to your place. That way you babysit for each other and if your friends live within walking distance, you can have a few drinks. Dress up, put fresh flowers, candles and napkins on the table for your 'guests' and drop friendly hints so that your 'hosts' know to make the same effort for you. Buy something from the local deli and a decent bottle of wine to take with you for your own supper. Don't answer the phone for your friends or watch their telly, try chatting to each other instead and see what happens.

85

Discover the joys of Tupperware parties and wife-swapping. (Yet another joke, I'm afraid.) I don't know what you get up to in your particular suburb, but in mine, we get our kicks from 'bring and share' lunches and suppers, where everyone contributes something – what the Americans call 'pot luck meals'. (I bet you're envious, aren't you?) More prudent Brits would probably prefer to assign dishes to participants, so as to avoid duplication. On the other hand, if you are happy to get six tiramisus but nothing savoury, throw caution to the wind and let people bring what they like.

86

Baby-sitting circles look enticingly cheap (i.e. free) but only join one if you really can't afford a baby-sitter. You will only end up resenting the Saturday evenings you spend, alone, watching someone else's telly while looking after their children, when you could be snuggled up in front of your own telly with your husband.

87 Loss of career status really gets to some non-working mothers. You have to grin and bear it for a while, but when you *do* get the time, try to find a way of using your professional skills, if only for a couple of hours a week. One woman I know runs a fortnightly French conversation group and another spends her Saturdays showing prospective buyers around houses for an estate agency. She tells me that the best bit is seeing how worn out her husband is after *just one day* with the kids. You may come home feeling nostalgic for the cut and thrust of working life – you may even feel thankful to be out of it.

Staying Sane

88 If you have always nursed a secret ambition to write a bodice-ripper, practise reflexology or design gardens, having children may actually kick-start it. Keep a small note book handy and jot down any ideas as they come to you. Motherhood may spell the end of one career, but it could launch you into another. Many women throw themselves with renewed vigour, wisdom and creativity into something new once their children go to school.

Staying Sane

89 Don't be tempted to recycle the bubble bath and aromatherapy oils you were given at Christmas. Keep them for yourself and luxuriate in a long hot bath once a month. Or once a week if you have time which, sadly, you won't.

90 Find, or invent, a parenting anecdote that you find funny each time you repeat it (and which you might even resort to when you feel like winding your children up.) I have a 'fun' wrist-watch with a bracelet made of blobs of fur, the shade of which matches *precisely* the colour of our hamster. Guess what I like to tell people?

91

Remember what you learnt from those Sunday school classes? Do something for someone else. Ask the old lady next door if she needs anything from the supermarket, invite a new Mum for coffee or offer to look after the child of a stressed-out friend (you'll find plenty). It's amazing how good you feel after a spot of altruism.

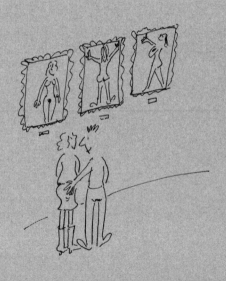

A Few Final Words of Wisdom

Nuggets to take or leave

Staying Sane

92 Ignore most parenting manuals (except this one, of course). They are usually too heavy to carry, too earnest to get through and their advice too bossy by half.

93 Keep your sense of humour, and when advice attacks you from all sides, trust your own instincts, not other people's.

94 Make friends with the ladies in your local charity shop. They are a wonderful source of toys, books and clothes for children. When your kids get wise, tell them it's important to learn the value of money.

95 Forget about being a domestic goddess. Your children would rather you spent more time with them and less time hoovering the hall or Dysoning the dining room.

Staying Sane

96 If you have a shed, lay claim to it before your husband does. You will find it invaluable for storing the exercise bike you keep planning to buy.

97 Never agree to look after another family's hamster while they're away. You'll only succumb to the pressure to buy one.

98
Invest in a fish tank-style lamp instead. The fish don't need feeding and it will take ages for your children to twig that they're plastic.

99
Make the most of your child-rearing years by remembering that although they seem to last forever, they are over all too quickly. And in your bleakest moments, hang on to the knowledge that one day, your children will remember the sacrifices you made to be with them. And if they don't, you can always remind them.

Epilogue

Why, despite all you have been through, you will probably want another baby

Because as a newborn, your child whined and howled for hours before puking all over you.

Because she kept you up all night, saw and heard you at your most desperate and wrecked your figure.

Because she drained you of your money and your energy, compromised your career prospects, interrupted every conversation and ruined every meal you tried to enjoy since she arrived.

Because as a toddler, she scribbled on the walls and broke several of your most treasured wedding-presents.

Because she pinched sweeties from Woolies, threw a tantrum at the hairdresser's and called your elderly neighbour 'a stinky poo'.

Because she insists on wearing shoes on the wrong feet and makes you snort with laughter during the vicar's sermon.

Because she wakes you up at the crack of dawn to demand you look for a threadbare nylon bunny and showers you with more love and affection than you thought you ever deserved.

Because your child makes her Daddy's eyes light up in a way that you never will and because, even when you've longed for a weekend away, you can't wait to get back and admire the gaudy pictures she has drawn for you.

Because your child is the best thing that ever happened to you.

Appendix

'The Good Wife's Guide', *Housekeeping Monthly*, May 1955

This wonderful reminder of a woman's domestic obligations purports to come from a 1950's American home economics magazine. In fact, it is more probable that it was written – as a spoof, I hope – in the 1970s, when it was circulated on University campuses.

Whatever its provenance, it made me laugh so much I nearly split my stitches.

Needless to say, I never forget to greet my husband without first washing the children's faces or tying a ribbon in my hair. And neither should you.

Have dinner ready. Plan ahead, even the night before, to have a delicious meal ready, on time for his return. This is a way of letting him know that you have been thinking about him and are concerned about his needs. Most men are hungry when they come home and the prospect of a good meal (especially his favourite dish) is part of the warm welcome needed.

Prepare yourself. Take 15 minutes to rest so you'll be refreshed when he arrives. Touch up your make-up, put a ribbon in your hair and be fresh-looking. He has just been with a lot of work-weary people.

Be a little gay and a little more interesting for him. His boring day may need a lift and one of your duties is to provide it.

Clear away the clutter. Make one last trip through the main part of the house just before your husband arrives.

Gather up schoolbooks, toys, paper, etc and then run a dustcloth over the tables.

Staying Sane

Over the cooler months of the year you should prepare and light a fire for him to unwind by. Your husband will feel he has reached a haven of rest and order, and it will give you a lift too. After all, catering for his comfort will provide you with immense personal satisfaction.

Prepare the children. Take a few minutes to wash the children's hands and faces (if they are small), comb their hair and, if necessary, change their clothes. They are little treasures and he would like to see them playing the part. Minimise all noise. At the time of his arrival, eliminate all noise of the washer, dryer, or vacuum. Try to encourage the children to be quiet.

Be happy to see him.

Greet him with a warm smile and show sincerity in your desire to please him.

Listen to him. You may have a dozen important things to tell him, but the moment of his arrival is not the time. Let him talk first — remember, his topics of conversation are more important than yours.

Make the evening his. Never complain if he comes home late or goes out to dinner, or other places of entertainment without you. Instead, try to understand his world of strain and pressure and his very real need to be at home and relax.

Your goal: Try to make sure your home is a place of peace, order, and tranquility where your husband can renew himself in body and spirit.

Don't greet him with complaints or problems.

Don't complain if he's late home for dinner or even if he stays out all night. Count this as minor compared to what he might have gone through that day.

Staying Sane

Make him comfortable. Have him lean back in a comfortable chair or have him lie down in the bedroom. Have a cool or warm drink ready for him.

Arrange his pillow and offer to take off his shoes. Speak in a low, soothing and pleasant voice.

Don't ask him questions about his actions or question his judgment or integrity. Remember, he is the master of the house and as such will always exercise his will with fairness and truthfulness. You have no right to question him.

A good wife always knows her place.